eatshop los angeles 3rd edition

an encapsulated view of the most interesting, inspired and authentic
locally owned eating and shopping establishments in los angeles, california

researched, photographed and written by anna h. blessing

cabazon books : 2010

table of contents

eat

shop

anna's notes on los angeles

I love a good makeover, and Los Angeles is the place for one. Anyone can become anything here, and finding yourself might mean a personal transformation that happens again and again and again. Transformation, evolution, metamorphosis—whatever you call it, it happens at lightspeed in this city—to both people and places (shops and restaurants most definitely included).

This is the third edition of *eat.shop los angeles*, and the first I have authored. Since Kaie (who writes some guest blurbs here—look for her initial "K") and Agnes's editions were released (in 2004 and 2007), much has changed. It's true that Tinseltown has plenty of glitz and glam, and some places even manage to live up to their media hype. But there are many more places that are below the radar, tucked away in lesser-known neighborhoods, oozing with authenticity. I hope you'll enjoy exploring the places I think make this city full of energy, creativity and lots of good eating and shopping.

Though shops and eateries are one of the best ways to get to know a city, sometimes our bellies and our wallets need a break. Here are a few of my favorite, quintessential L.A. activites:

1 > *Eames House*: Walk around the exterior and peek through the windows to check out Charles and Ray's home in its original state.

2 > *Hollywood Farmer's Market*: Okay, so technically this is both eating and shopping, but compelling enough to also be sight-seeing.

3 > *Yoga at Golden Bridge*: A physical and spiritual experience not to be missed if you really want a dose of L.A. living.

4 > *Thai massage at Pho Siam*: You're going to need this after the yoga. Make it a theme day and stop by *Pho Café* for a bowl of goodness afterward.

5 > *The Getty Museum*: Views, architecture and art at Richard Meier's glowing white structure.

about eat.shop

• All of the businesses featured in this book are locally owned. In deciding which businesses to feature, that's our number one criteria. Then we look for businesses that strike us as utterly authentic and uniquely conceived, whether they be new or old, chic or funky. And if you were wondering, businesses don't pay to be featured—that's not our style!

• A note about our maps. They are stylized, meaning they don't show every street. If you'd like a more detailed map, pick up a Streetwise map for Los Angeles or we have an online map with the indicators of the businesses noted > map.eatshopguides.com/la3. And a little note about exploring a city. The businesses we feature are mainly in neighborhoods within the urban core. Each of these 'hoods (and others that we don't cover) have dozens of great stores and restaurants other than the ones listed in this book.

• Make sure to double check the hours of the business before you go as they often change seasonally.

• The pictures and descriptions for each business are meant to give you the feel for a place. Don't be upset with the business if what you see or read is no longer available.

• Small local businesses have always had to work that much harder to keep their heads above water. During these rough economic times, some will close. Does this mean the book is no longer valid? Absolutely not! The more you use this book and visit these businesses, the better chance they have to stay open!

• The *eat.shop* clan consists of a small crew of creative types who travel extensively and have dedicated themselves to great eating and interesting shopping around the world. Each of these people writes, photographs and researches his or her own books, and though they sometimes do not live in the city of the book they author, they draw from a vast network of local sources to deepen the well of information used to create the guides.

• Please support the indie bookstores in Los Angeles. To find these bookstores, use this great source: www.indiebound.org/indie-store-finder.

• *eat.shop* supports the *3/50 project* (www.the350project.net) and in honor of it have begun our own challenge (please see the back inside cover of this book).

• There are three ranges of prices noted for restaurants, $ = cheap, $$ = medium, $$$ = expensive

• Kaie Wellman, creator of the *eat.shop guides* writes a couple of blurbs in the books noted as "K".

previous edition businesses

If you own the prevous editions of *eat.shop los angeles*, make sure to keep them. Think of each edition as part of an overall "volume" of books, as many of the businesses not featured in this new edition are still fantastic. The reason earlier edition businesses aren't in this book is because there are so many amazing businesses that deserve a chance to be featured!

eat

3 square cafe
alcove cafe & bakery
alegria on sunset
auntie em's kitchen
baby blues bar-b-q
beechwood
blair's
bld
bluebird café
bob's coffee and donuts
casbah cafe
cafe mimosa
cafe nagomi
cafe tropical
chameau
chez jay
colorado wine company
delilah bakery
dominick's
empanada's place
ford's filling station
gingergrass
graffeo
inaka
izayoi
jin patisserie
la serenata de garibaldi
little next door

lou
magnolia
malibu seafood
manpuku
mao's kitchen
mashti malone's
mexico city
milk
moishe's
musso & frank grill
pace
pacific dining car
port royal
silverlake wine
square one dining
stroh's gourmet
the cheese store of
beverly hills
the cheese store of
silverlake
singapore's banana leaf
the arsenal
sona
the gumbo pot
the hungry cat
the oinkster
via cafe
vincenti ristorante

shop

a + r
blends / 06+
calleen cordero
carol young undesigned
des kohan
distant
dosa818
family
flounce vintage
gypsy's palace
healing waters
hillary rush
keep
le pink
loft appeal
marie mason
pamela barish
panty raid
particolare
patio culture
persimmon
planet maple board shop
sonrisa
soolip
reserve
salt
scent bar
scout

show
surfas
10 ten
the stronghold 1895
turpan
union
weego home
yolk

if a previous edition business does not appear on this list, it is either featured again in this edition, has closed or no longer meets our criteria or standards.

where to lay your weary head

there are many great places to stay in los angeles, but here are a few of my picks:

maison 140
140 lasky drive (beverly hills)
310.281.4000 / maison140beverlyhills.com
standard double from $150 restaurant: bar noir
notes: intimate boutique hotel, kelly wearstler-style

the london
1020 north san vicente boulevard (west hollywood)
866.282.4560 / thelondondwesthollywood.com
standard double from $249 restaurants: boxwood cafe, gordon ramsay
notes: big and beautiful with a rooftop pool

palihouse
8465 holloway drive (west hollywood)
323.656.4100 / palihouse.com
standard double from $200 restaurant: manny's
notes: mod all-suite urban lodge

the charlie hotel
819 north sweetzer avenue (west hollywood)
310.927.9307 / thecharliehotel.com
call for rates
notes: your own private english bungalow

the ambrose
1255 20th street (santa monica)
310.315.1555 / ambrosehotel.com
standard double from $150
notes: holistic hospitality

hotel erwin
1697 pacific avenue (venice)
310.452.1111 / jdvhotels.com/hotels/losangeles/erwin
standard double from $169 restaurant: hash
notes: california casual at the beach

notes

angelini osteria

simple, sublime italian

7313 beverly boulevard. between fuller and pointsettia
323.297.0070 www.angeliniosteria.com
lunch tue - fri noon - 2:30p dinner tue - sun 5:30 - 10:30p

opened in 1997. owner / chef: gino angelini
$$-$$$: all major credit cards accepted
lunch. dinner. reservations accepted

mid-city > **e01**

Common to Los Angeles are large-scale restaurants with sometimes over-the-top décor, high attention to image and only second, or sometimes third-degree attention to the food itself. It's with supreme pleasure then to go to a place like *Angelini Osteria*, where the atmosphere is intimate yet no-nonsense, and one hundred percent of the attention and focus is put on the food. This seminal Italian restaurant was featured in the first *eat.shop los angeles* for good reason, and it continues to win us over years later, and will continue to for years to come.

imbibe / devour:
felsina chianti classico riserva
fresh anchovies with artichokes & red beets
pumpkin tortelli
lasagna verde "omaggio nonna elvira"
whole branzino
breaded veal chop ala milanese
arugula, mozzarella & prosciutto piadina
burrata & tomato pizza

animal

like nothing else in los angeles

435 north fairfax avenue. between rosewood and oakwood
323.782.9225 www.animalrestaurant.com
sun - thu 6 - 11p fri - sat 6p - 2a

opened in 2008. owner / chefs: jon shook and vinny dotolo
$$: all major credit cards accepted
dinner. late night

mid-city > e02

Right around the time I was first heading to *Animal*, I was on the fence of vegetarianism, checking out the greener grass on the other side of the pig pen. If there is anywhere that has me hopping back in the pen, it's *Animal*. Crisp pig ear with chili and lime! Sweetbreads and creamed spinach! Ribs and rabbit, foie gras and oxtail. Eating here is a brilliant study on how delicious the animal can be, from head to tail. And if you would prefer not to eat animals, one of my favorite delights here is the delicious gnocchi. Regardless of which side of the fence you sit on, *Animal* is the place to be.

imbibe / devour:
06 baxter henneberg vineyard pinot noir
little yella pils
pig ear, chili, lime, fried egg
barbeque pork belly sandwiches
ricotta & goat cheese gnocchi
pork belly, kimchi, peanuts, chili, soy, scallion
ribeye for two
tres leches, dulce de leche

axe

classic california cuisine

1009 abbot kinney boulevard. between brooks and broadway
310.664.9787 www.axerestaurant.com
see website for hours

opened in 1999. owner / chef: joanna moore
$$: all major credit cards accepted
lunch. dinner. brunch. reservations accepted

venice > e03

In this spread out city, people stick to their side of town. You know, birds of a feather flock together. If you live in Venice, you rarely travel to Silverlake. If Highland Park is home, you probably don't spend a lot of time in Brentwood. There are rare birds, though, who will go anywhere and everywhere. Within this species is the *Axe* bird. She might live on the east side, but *Axe* in Venice is still her favorite restaurant in town. This is not a rare bird—*Axe* is hugely beloved—which is the reason that this spot is showing up for a third time in this book. Which makes me a member of the flock.

imbibe / devour:
lemonade
hot cocoa
composed salad plate
mediterranean tuna salad
grilled swiss gruyère sandwich
spicy chicken soup
basic rice bowl
homemade ice cream

bay cities

old-school italian deli and market
1517 lincoln boulevard. between broadway and colorado
310.395.8279 www.bcdeli.com
tue - sat 9a - 7p sun 9a - 6p

opened in 1925
$: visa. mc
grocery. deli. first come, first served

santa monica > **e04**

Have you ever tried to smuggle in a hunk of Parmiggiano Reggiano from a trip to Italy? A bottle of divine olive oil? A favorite tin of licorices bought at a corner tabac? My hand is raised; I'm a smuggler. But I'm going straight now that I have *Bay Cities*. Most people come here for one of their massive and oft-praised sandwiches from the deli—but the line can be long, so grab a ticket and start your shopping while you wait to place your order. You'll find the market is just as great as the sandwiches. Just be sure to snag a sandwich either way—these big beauties are good enough to smuggle across borders.

imbibe / devour:
olive oils & vinegars
parmiggiano reggiano
glazed & roasted figs
from the deli:
  artichokes
  copa seca
  bresaola
  sandwiches!

ARTICHOKES	4 98	BREASOLA	6 98
CAPONATA	9 98	CAPI COLA	6 98
CAPRESE	9 98	CHICKEN	8 98
CHICKEN SALAD	7 98	COPA SECA	
COLESLAW	2 49	CORNED BEEF	8 98
CUCUMBER	5 98	HAM	5 98
		BOILED	
EGGPLANT ROUND		BLACK FOREST / HONEY BAKED	8 98
FOUR BEAN P	3 49	LOW SALT	
GARBANZO P	3 49	JAMON SRNO 23 98
		LIVERWURST	4 98

best fish taco in ensenada

the name says it all

1650 north hillhurst avenue. between prospect and sunset
323.466.5552 www.bestfishtacoinensenada.com
daily 11a - 8:30p

opened in 2007. owner: joseph cordova
$: cash only
lunch. dinner. first come, first served

los feliz >

Here's what I think. If someone says they have the best of something, for example, a fish taco—I immediately assume the opposite. But this place with the boasty name of *Best Fish Taco in Ensenada* is not bragging without merit. Here's the menu: Fish. Shrimp. Drink. Seems simple, but there's a lot of energy and care and damn good ingredients that go into making this food. To heighten the experience, make sure to load up at the creative salsa bar. And though the name is not *Best Fish Taco and Horchata in Ensenada*, the horchata here takes a prize as well—made Guatemalan style—it's delish.

imbibe / devour:
horchata
tacos:
  fish
  shrimp
salsa bar:
  radish relish
  la crema magica
  hot guac

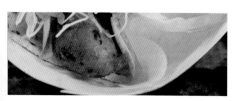

17

café de leche

a south american-inspired café

5000 york boulevard. corner of north avenue 50
323.551.6828 www.cafedeleche.net
daily 7a - 7p

opened in 2008. owners: matt and anya schodorff
$: all major credit cards accepted
coffee / tea. snacks. first come, first served

highland park > **e06**

Part of the fun of L.A. can certainly be "the scene," which is nearly impossible to avoid if you're going out and about eating and drinking. But unless you are a complete scene-a-phant, there are times when you need to get away from the scariness and find a quiet place where people go to actually drink coffee. *Café de Leche* is one of these no-nonsense, settle in with your newspaper and enjoy a good cup of coffee spots. I dare you to spot a posturer who's scanning the room behind dark shades. Go ahead and breathe in the fresh, attitude-free air around you. Ahhhhhhh...

imbibe / devour:
horchata with espresso
organic agave mocha
organic mate latte
organic hot chocolate
banana nut muffin
dulce de leche kiss
cheese pastry
milca soda roja

HIGHLAND PA

canelé

farmer's market fresh food

3219 glendale boulevard. between brunswick and edenhurst
323.666.7133 www.canele-la.com
see website for hours

opened in 2006. owner / chef: corina weibel owner: jane choi
$$-$$$: all major credit cards accepted
dinner. brunch. first come, first served

atwater village > **e07**

Sometimes when you go out to eat, do you secretly hope the food is going to taste like a delicious home-cooked meal? So why not then just stay at home and cook? Because few of us can cook a meal the way we idealize it to taste, so we search for the someone who can. Corina at *Canelé* is that someone. Take her roast chicken or her three-egg omelette— simple, perfectly executed and deliciously fulfilling food that is the essence of a "home-cooked meal." The only problem here is this: which to order first, the chicken or the egg?

imbibe / devour:
concord grape mimosa
lamill coffee
pecan sticky bun
baked pancake
persimmon salad
eggs en cocotte
open-faced blt
fried chicken sandwich

carmela ice cream

fresher-than-fresh ice cream
farmer's markets throughout los angeles
323.319.6084 www.carmelaicecream.com
check website for hours and locations

opened in 2007. owners: zachary cox and jessica mortarotti
$: all major credit cards accepted
treats. first come, first served

roaming >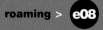

When I first became pregnant, everybody wanted to know what my cravings were. Did I crave the stereo-typical pickles and ice cream? Pickles yes, ice cream no. Then I met *Carmela*. *Carmela* the ice cream, that is. I have a feeling that this new craving has nothing to do with hormones and everything to do with how insanely delicious this ice cream is. Selling their delights at various farmer's markets about town, Zach and Jessica use farm-fresh produce to flavor this delicious frozen delight. I wonder what my excuse to eat it to excess will be once I can no longer blame the bun-in-the-oven.

imbibe / devour:
ice cream:
    salted caramel
    dark chocolate with cacao nibs
    brown sugar vanilla bean
sorbet:
    lemon basil
    cucumber
    citrus

church & state

industrial chic bistro

1850 industrial street. between sixth and seventh
213.405.1434 www.churchandstatebistro.com
see website for hours

opened in 2008. owner: yasmin sarmadi chef: walter manzke
$$-$$$: all major credit cards accepted
lunch. dinner. reservations recommended

downtown >  **e09**

People often use geographical references to describe the places where they eat. For example, if a restaurant in Chicago reminds me of one that could be found in the Pacific Northwest city I grew up in, I call it Portland-y. Admit it, everybody plays this game because it helps to define the feel of a place. I found myself doing this with *Church & State*. It feels nothing like L.A., and much more like New York, or scratch that, a mix of New York and Paris. With its bistro atmosphere, well-researched French menu and a chef who's got the magic touch—I guess I should say that it feels most like Heaven.

imbibe / devour:
ginger grape press
champagne cocktail
escargots de bourgogne
assiette de charcuterie
tarte flambée
jambon & beurre sandwich
omelette forestière
pot de crème au chocolat

clementine

bakery and cafe

1751 ensley avenue. between eastborne and santa monica
310.552.1080 www.clementineonline.com
mon - fri 7a - 7:30p sat 8a - 5p

opened in 2000. owner / chef: annie miller
$-$$: all major credit cards accepted
breakfast. lunch. dinner. treats. first come, first served

century city > **e10**

This is a case of OSKB (Older Sister Knows Best). When I first started working on this book, my sister wouldn't stop talking about her love of *Clementine*. I tuned her out (as sisters do) as *Clementine* had been in the first edition of this book, and I was sure there were scads of places that had eclipsed it. But after I'd eaten my way through many like-minded spots throughout the city, I kept coming back here because their baked goods are matchless and, more importantly, because they celebrate "Grilled Cheese Month." So with tail between my legs, I admit to you, dear sister: *Clementine* rocks.

imbibe / devour:
fresh-squeezed ginger limeade
café latte
tuna melt
meatloaf sandwich
granola
two hot buttermilk biscuits
banana cake
cinnamon rolls

coolhaus

mobile modern ice cream
roaming locations
www.eatcoolhaus.com
check website for hours and locations

opened in 2009. owners: natasha case and freye estreller
$: cash only
treats. first come, first served

roaming > **e11**

I have an admission. For awhile, I was a *Coolhaus* stalker. I tracked them on Twitter, trying to line up my daily schedule with their truck whereabouts. Time after time, I missed the truck by minutes—held up in traffic or on the other side of the city. Then one golden day everything came together, and I had my first encounter with one of their ice cream sandwiches—the mint and chocolate combo—as I had planned my menu decision weeks before. It was worth the hunt. Like the holy grail in Indiana Jones, these treats might grant you eternal life or, at the very least, some substantial happiness.

imbibe / devour:
ice cream sandwiches:
   rem coolhaus
   richard meyer lemon
   mies vanilla rohe
   mintimalism
   eric owenmeal matcha
   mini case study pack
   or make your own!

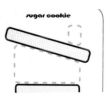

daikokuya

ramen, ramen, ramen!
327 east first street. between san pedro and alameda
213.626.1680 www.daikoku-ten.com
mon - thu 11a - midnight fri - sat 11a - 1a sun noon - when soup is gone

$: visa. mc
lunch. dinner. late night. first come, first served

little tokyo >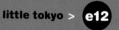

K: What is a ramenhead? It's a person who spits on the ground when the words "Top Ramen" are uttered. This someone also belongs to ramen chat rooms and endlessly discusses the best ramen spots in a city, what their soup bases are made out of and the texture of the noodles. Though I love the stuff, alas, I am no ramenhead. Unfortunately, the last ramen I ate tasted like a bowl of barnyard. Memorable, though not delicious. The ramen at *Daikokuya* is both—with its rich broth, slices of pork belly, chijuri-style egg noodles and a marinated boiled egg bobbing about. Yum.

imbibe / devour:
oolong shochu
ramune soda
gyoza
tsukemono
sliced kurabota pork belly
daikoku ramen
tsukemen ramen
shredded pork belly

el huarache azteca

home of the huarache
5225 york boulevard. between north ave 52 and north ave 53
323.478.9572 daily 8am - 10:30pm

$: cash only
breakfast. lunch. dinner. first come, first served

highland park > **e13**

I remember the first time I ate at a dive. It was in high school, and I was with an adventurous friend. I eyed the peeling paint, what looked like a shady clientele and the perceived scary menu. I was petrified. Since that time I've learned that peeling paint is really "patina," that shady clientele are often food-loving insiders who want to keep their gem a secret and that scary menus often feature amazing food. So I love *El Huarache Azteca*. I devoured the huaraches (Mexican pizzas), dousing everything with salsas from the (seemingly shady) salsa bar. I love this dive, peeling paint and all.

imbibe / devour:
jamaica agua fresca
horchata
consomme de borrego
chilaquiles
veggie torta
huaraches:
  pork adobada
  carne asada

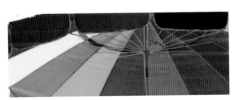

food + lab

organic, european cafe
7253 santa monica boulevard. between fuller and formosa
323.851.7120 www.foodlabcatering.com
daily 8a - 8p

opened in 2009. owners: nino and esther linsmayer
$-$$: all major credit cards accepted
breakfast. lunch. dinner. first come, first served

west hollywood > **e14**

Years ago I visited a beautiful mountain town on the border of Italy and Austria called Bolzano. This place was a wonderful mash-up of Italian food, wine and beautiful scenery with the organized, solid design sense of the Austrians. Two diverse cultures blending together. This is the case with *Food + Lab*, where the SoCal menu is injected with Austrian specialties, like muesli, home-made Austrian meatloaf and Vienna Kaffee. The focus is organic, fresh food and the market shelves are stocked with specialty foodstuffs, local and imported alike. This melting pot makes up one tasty place.

imbibe / devour:
alm dudler soda
imported nutella
deluscious cookies
housemade swiss bircher muesli with berries
belgian waffle with orange compote
fingerling potatoes, caramelized onion,
   gruyère & bacon
prosciutto & fresh fig sandwich

fugetsu-do

japanese confectionary and bakery
315 east first street. between san pedro and alameda
213.625.8595 www.fugetsu-do.com
sun - thu 8a - 6p fri - sat 8a - 7p

opened in 1903. owner: brian s. kito
$: cash only
treats. first come, first served

little tokyo >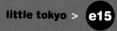

K: I seem to have mochi on the mind these days. Just a couple of months ago I shot *Benkyo-do* for the new *eat.shop san francisco*. I must admit I'm a little worried though about *Benkyo-do's* experience level. After all, they've only been around since 1906. *Fugetsu-do* has been in business since 1903, which makes this small store the grandaddy of American mochi makers. Though many Americans know mochi because it's sprinkled on their fro-yo, don't let that be the only way you experience this Japanese confection. There are many varieties and flavors, each one tastier than the next.

imbibe / devour:
mochi:
  strawberry anco
  yakiman
  inaka
  sudare
  ogura
  rainbow dango
  mikan

gjelina

rustic american food that draws crowds

1429 abbot kinney boulevard. corner of milwood
310.450.1429 www.gjelina.com
mon - fri 11:30a - midnight sat - sun 10:30a - midnight brunch until 3p

opened in 2008. owner / chef: travis lett
$$: all major credit cards accepted
lunch. dinner. brunch. reservations recommended

venice > **e16**

Gjelina is a beautiful restaurant. Though a gorgeous girl might be one in a million in this city, a beautiful restaurant here is a bird of a different feather. From the etched wall carvings to the vintage wood and metal school chairs to the rough-hewn center table and the quirky lightbulb chandelier to big bowls filled with orange tomatoes and figs. But *Gjelina* is more than just a pretty face; the food is substantial and prepared with precision. Smart, pretty and delicious. I think *Gjelina* might be lust at first sight, love at first taste.

imbibe / devour:
the visionary cocktail
pappardelle with spicy tomato, anchovy,
    breadcrumbs & parmesan
farro, squash & kale soup
pizzas:
    hen of the woods mushroom & beet greens
    guanciale, crushed olives & mozzarella
    lamb sausage, rapini, tomato confit & asiago

good girl dinette

vietnamese comfort food

110 north avenue 56. between figueroa and marmion
323.257.8980 www.goodgirldinette.com
tue - thu 5:30 - 9:30p fri 5:30 - 10p sat noon - 10p sun noon - 9p

opened in 2009. owner / chef: diep tran
$$: visa. mc
lunch. dinner. reservations accepted

highland park > **e17**

The last time I ate a chicken pot pie I was probably in junior high, and it was the tin-lined, frozen variety with chunky peas and carrots and dry chicken. Not exactly gourmet, but comforting and strangely delicious all the same. When I spotted the chicken pot pie on the menu at *Good Girl Dinette*, I decided it was time for a re-visit. I think it was the best thing I had eaten in weeks, maybe months. I sat there and blew on the still-hot bites, unable to stop devouring the curry-rich chicken and perfect crust. Pot pie paradise can be yours at *Good Girl Dinette*.

imbibe / devour:
housemade sodas
vietnamese-style coffee
rice cakes with crispy scallion tofu
slow-roasted pork baguette
grandpa's porridge
chicken pot pie
eggplant curry
lattice-top pie

joan's on third

beloved cafe and market

8350 west third street. between orlando and sweetzer
323.655.2285 www.joansonthird.com
mon - sat 8a - 8p sun 8a - 6p

opened in 1998. owner: joan mcnamara
$$: all major credit cards accepted
breakfast. lunch. dinner. grocery. first come, first served

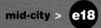

mid-city > **e18**

Sometimes these books are about heralding the unknown. And sometimes they are about praising the quintessential places in a city. *Joan's on Third* is the latter. I doubt there's a person in this town who doesn't know—and already love—this pretty and pristine café and market. It's a hangout for friends, a huge help for hosting parties (the sharply edited cheese selection alone is reason to make a trip), and an all-around fantastic place to grab darn good food any time of day. Even after my research was over, I found myself returning to *Joan's* regularly, along with the rest of L.A.

imbibe / devour:
cappuccino
fresh fruit smoothie
soft-boiled organic farm egg
chocolate french toast
chinese chicken salad
five-herb whole roasted chicken
snap peas with asparagus & shallots
chocolate covered marshmallow cloud cupcake

la estrella

my favorite taco truck
corner of york and avenue 54
24/7

$: cash only
lunch. dinner. first come, first served

highland park > **e19**

Many Los Angelenos will tell you their favorite taco can be found at a taco truck, and if you talk to folks about where their favorite one is, you'll hear a zillion different impassioned opinions about which truck is the best. So I'm going to give you my two cents. I'm picking and sticking to *La Estrella*. Yep, it's all the way out in Highland Park, but this truck is the taco jackpot, where the tortillas are loaded with juicy heaps of meat and the perfect kick of hot sauce. Sorry to say though that this truck doesn't travel—so you might have to break your own habit to visit here.

imbibe / devour:
sidral mundet
tacos:
  asada
  al pastor
  carnitas
  lengua
  caveza

45

lamill

serious coffee

1636 silver lake boulevard. corner of effie
323.663.4441 www.lamillcoffee.com
sun - thu 7a - 10p fri - sat 7a - 11p

opened in 2008. owners: craig and jean min
$: all major credit cards accepted
breakfast. lunch. coffee. first come, first served

silverlake > **e20**

In my current preggy state, I can take in stride the ever-expanding belly and the elimination of certain foods—cutting alcohol hasn't even gotten me down. But I deeply mourn the demise of my daily coffee habit. When I stopped into *Lamill* for breakfast once morning, I threw all discipline out the window and got the very largest coffee on the menu. I twitched with excitement as I watched it brew in front of me. When it came time to drink it, I relished every drop like it was liquid gold. And though my doctor might not have approved, my baby now knows what really good coffee is.

imbibe / devour:
coffee extractions:
  chemex
  siphon brew
  french press
house-made brioche doughnut holes
sofia panini
jambon de paris au beurre salé baguette
strawberry shortcake

lark cake shop

super sweet cake and cupcake shop

3337 west sunset boulevard. corner of micheltorena
323.667.2968 www.larkcakeshop.com
sun - mon noon - 6p tue - thu 10a - 8p fri - sat 10a - 10p

opened in 2007. owners: james and colleen standish
$-$$: all major credit cards accepted
treats. first come, first served

silverlake > e21

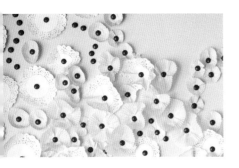

When I started working on this book, I would have sworn to you that I wouldn't put in a cupcake spot. It's not that I don't love a good cupcake, but cupcake places have multiplied like rabbits, and many are average at best. Then I discovered *Lark Cake Shop* which is truly special (technically, it's a cake and cupcake spot, so I felt like I wasn't breaking my early rule, btw). The edible gems here are just the right size, and perfectly moist with an appropriate frosting-to-cake ratio. And they've got nifty wrappers that make eating them oh, so easy to devour without a mess. I'm re-embracing the cupcake.

imbibe / devour:
cupcakes:
  sara's famous chocolate mousse
  carrot cake
  old-fashioned ice box
  colleen's caramel
  red velvet
  berry shortcake
  flourless chocolate

49

loteria! grill

regional mexican food

6627 hollywood boulevard. the farmers market. corner of third and fairfax
see website for other locations
www.loteriagrill.com
mon - sat 9a - 9p sun 9a - 7p

opened in 2002. owner / chef: jimmy shaw
$: all major credit cards accepted
breakfast. lunch. dinner. first come, first served

mid-city >

Don't get me wrong; I think the food truck craze that has descended on this city is a good thing (see *La Estrella*). But when I don't feel like eating great Mexican fare standing out in the elements or slopping food around my car, *Loteria Grill* is my spot of choice. The way I see this place is that it's the best of both worlds. There's great interior Mexican cuisine, but with a lot more menu choices AND a place to sit. Then for bonus points, you get to soak up the always entertaining, sometimes circus-like atmosphere of the Farmers Market. It's a win-win.

imbibe / devour:
watermelon agua fresca
café de olla
nachos
tacos:
  nopalitos
  cochinita pibil
  carne deshebrada
  pollo en pipian rojo

mendocino farms

drool-worthy sandwiches

300 south grand avenue. corner of third
444 flower street. corner of fifth
213.620.1114 / 213.627.3262 www.mendocinofarms.com
mon - fri 11a - 3p

opened in 2005. owner: mario del pero
$: all major credit cards accepted
lunch. first come, first served

downtown >

People like to gripe about driving in L.A. Seems a bit to me like living in Minnesota and complaining about the snow, but I guess people need something to complain about. In talking about *Mendocino Farms*, I often heard from people, "It's supposed to be amazing, but I'm not driving downtown for a sandwich." Still, I decided to take the journey. I got stuck in traffic and then couldn't find a parking spot. I began to silently gripe. But when I wrapped my mouth around the Rustic California sandwich—I can tell you that gridlock never tasted so good. Be brave; make the drive.

imbibe / devour:
galvanina blood orange soda
sandwiches:
    highway 128
    curry chicken salad
    rustic california
    kurobuta pork belly banh mi
    cubana americano italiano
housemade pickles

mo-chica

contemporary peruvian
3655 south grand avenue. between 36th and 37th
213.747.2141 www.mo-chica.com
mon - sat lunch 11a - 4p dinner 6 - 11p

opened in 2009. owner / chef: ricardo zarate
$$: cash only
lunch. dinner. first come, first served

downtown >

K: Though over the years I have perfected the art of cool nonchalance, I still enjoy a good gush. And when somebody, something or someplace makes me want to gush, then I just let it all hang out. I love *Mo-Chica*. Located in a funky food court, this place is truly off-the-beaten-path unless you go to USC or live/work downtown. But don't let this get in your way as this is a place to make tracks to. Ricardo, who is Lima-born and London-trained, makes the most exquisite modern Peruvian food. I was so high with pleasure after eating here, my husband thought I was on drugs. I was—the *Mo-Chica* drug.

imbibe / devour:
purple corn ice tea
barley ice tea with ginger & herbs
ceviche del dia
causa
papa a la huancaina
quinotto
aji de gallina
seco de cordero

nickel diner

a new kind of diner

524 south main street. between fifth and sixth
213.623.8301 www.nickeldiner.com
breakfast + lunch tue - sun 8a - 3:30p dinner tue - sat 6 - 11p

opened in 2008. owner: kristin trattner chef: monica may pastry chef: sharlena fong
$-$$: all major credit cards accepted
breakfast. lunch. dinner. first come, first served

downtown > **e25**

Sometimes there's an item that I've eaten that stands out against all the other things I've stuck in my gullet while working on a book. In L.A., the winner was the crunchy coated strawberry doughnut at *Nickel Diner*. It's so darn tasty, so totally dessert-for-breakfast, that it feels like a food item a kid would create in his imagination—a food that an adult would scoff at. So for all the kids out there stuck in grown-up bodies, get yourself to *Nickel Diner* for one of these crazy good doughnuts. I'd recommend eating dessert first in this case.

imbibe / devour:
old-fashioned sodas
egg mcnickel
dutch baby pancake
smac & cheese
niteclub sandwich
mama's spaghetti & meatballs
peanut butter potato chip cupcake
homemade ding-dongs

nook bistro

tucked away bistro

11628 santa monica boulevard #9. between barry and federal
310.207.5160 www.nookbistro.com
see website for hours

opened in 2004. owner / chef: james richardson
owners: jeff stuppler and brian frith-smith
$$: all major credit cards accepted
lunch. dinner. reservations accepted

west los angeles > **e26**

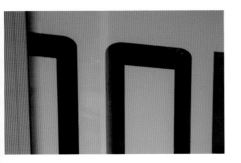

"Fine dining in a strip mall," I thought, "no way." But as the saying goes, you can't judge a book by its cover, *Nook Bistro* being the book, strip mall being the cover. This Nook is literal. It is in a little corner of the aforementioned strip mall, surrounded by neighboring businesses that wouldn't have much in common with it other than their addresses. With a menu of modern comfort food and so many things that sound delicious, it's painful having to decide what to order. I can think of worse problems, but I can't think of a better place to eat than here.

imbibe / devour:
ommegang hennepin farmhouse ale
08 castelo de medina verdejo
new zealand green lip mussels
cornershop caesar
nook burger
chicken paillard
squash & chickpea stew
chocolate & banana bread pudding

palate food + wine

restaurant and wine bar with amazing eats

933 south brand boulevard. between acacia and garfield
818.662.9463 www.palatefoodwine.com
see website for hours

opened in 2008. owner / chef: octavio becerra owner: steve goldun
$$-$$$: all major credit cards accepted
dinner. lunch. reservations accepted

glendale >

I've always been better at baking than cooking, thanks to my aptitude for precision, and no thanks to my lack of talent for winging it. If, however, I could cook with great skill, I would want to make the kind of food Octavio makes at *Palate*. I found myself taking notes not just for this book, but for my own personal uses—wondering if I could recreate the sweet potato gnocchi with sage, celery and chestnuts, with a light grating of spicy pecans on top to give it a kick. In the long run I think I'll stick to my quick breads and pizza dough, and let the experts at *Palate* do the cooking.

imbibe / devour:
08 domaine la bastide viognier
07 organic fouquet vouvray sec le marigny
pickled turnip & beets
porkfolio
potted lamb
monkfish with spiced mussels &
  bloomsdale spinach
warm tarte flambée

pho café

a place for pho and vietnamese home cooking
2841 west sunset boulevard. at silver lake boulevard
213.413.0888
daily 11a - midnight

owner: cindy dam
$-$$: cash only
lunch. dinner. first come, first served

silverlake > **e28**

My friend Annie likes to give specific, ornately detailed food descriptions. Not only will she regale you with the 10 things she loves on any given menu, she can also list the 12 things she has tried and is not so excited about. To add to her L.A. eating cred, there's almost nowhere in this town she hasn't eaten. So, when she casually mentioned to me that the Vietnamese crepe at *Pho Café* was maybe her favorite menu item anywhere in town, I was on my way before she could finish her sentence. Though Annie can exaggerate a bit, this crepe wasn't unfairly hyped. It was crazy good.

imbibe / devour:
vietnamese coffee
33 beer
fresh homemade limeade
goi cuon
banh xeo
pho tai
pho tai bo vien
bun cha gio

reddi-chick

b.b.q. chicken and ribs
225 26th street. in the brentwood country mart
310.393.5238
mon - sat 9a - 8p

opened about 35 years ago. owners: steve and carol salita
$: cash only
breakfast. lunch. dinner. first come, first served

brentwood >

This is the story of "Anna's Great Roast Chicken Quest." I spent a full day eating roasty birds all over this metropolis because L.A. is a roast chicken-obsessed town. What did I learn on my quest? That I did not develop feathers, as I worried I might, and that I had a serious preference for *Reddi-Chick*. Yes folks, even though it's been around forever (this chick has been around the block) and brags a host of crazy loyal fans, I believe *Reddi-Chick* deserves a blue ribbon for taking the cake… or, er, is it the egg? Either way, get your roasted, rotisserie chick here.

imbibe / devour:
chicken basket
chicken wing & rib basket
chicken tender basket
whole chicken
side bbq ribs
cole slaw
baked beans
french fries

samosa house and bharat bazaar

vegetarian indian cuisine and market

11510 west washington boulevard. between mclaughlin and sawtelle
310.398.6766 www.samosahouse.net
daily 10:30a - 9:30p

opened in 1979. owners: vibha and kunal bhojak
$: all major credit cards accepted
lunch. dinner. grocery. first come, first served

culver city >

I have a fantasy of living in the India described by the classic English novelists. I would take pleasure rides on elephants, lounge in the shade under a big fan whilst reading and eat great feasts served in beautiful and ornate dishes. While this is one fantasy that won't come true, I can work on fulfilling a portion of it at *Samosa House*, namely: made-to-order samosas, fresh mango lassis and various vessels to take home and serve my Indian feast in if I'm so inclined. To really feel like a Brit living overseas in India, I'll pick up some English tea. I'll be that much closer to living the dream.

imbibe / devour:
mango lassi
rose milk
samosas
saag
chana masala
okra - bhindi
rajma dal
british sweets & cookies

scoops

housemade ice cream with flavors that change daily

712 north heliotrope drive. at melrose
323.906.2649
mon - sat noon - 10p sun 2 - 6p

opened in 2004. owner: tai kim
$: cash only
treats. first come, first served

mid-wilshire > e31

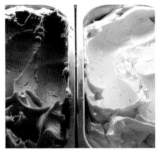

A cop, a hipster, two businessmen, a bike messenger and me. What food and place could attract such a wide variety of people and palates? Ice cream at *Scoops*. Why here: There's a varietal cornucopia of ice cream made fresh here daily, from simple, yet unusual flavours such as salt and honey to the outré green tea and ricotta cheese. With all this to choose from, I had a root beer float. Sounds boring to you? Try it with Virgil's root beer and brown bread ice cream. At *Scoops*, there is something for everyone. Just don't get your heart set on anything because it will be gone tomorrow.

imbibe / devour:
brown bread & virgil's root beer float
ice cream & sorbets:
  blackberry jasmine
  coconut lemongrass
  guinness & tiramisu
  salt & honey
  lychee pear
  pear & riesling

shima

heart·healthy sushi

1432 abbot kinney boulevard. between navarre and palms
310.314.0882
tue - sat 5:30 - 10:30p

opened in 2004. owner / chef: yoshi shima
$$-$$$: all major credit cards accepted
dinner. reservations accepted

venice >

Not that it was ever a consideration, but doing this book without featuring a great sushi place would be like doing the Chicago book without a pizza place. Is it a problem to find a fantastic sushi place in this town? No, as there are a number of them (*Kiyokawa* for example). But is there a place that's a true original? Yes, *Shima*. Aside from offering top-notch fish, the focus here is on being as healthful as possible using brown rice, divine housemade tofu and no non-fish animal fats. This creates a menu that is as good for you as it is good to eat and is quintessentially L.A.

imbibe / devour:
nigori with pomegranate
brown rice green tea
organic homemade tofu
kelp shooter
japanese aji spanish mackerel sashimi
japanese octopus carpaccio
baby halibut sashimi
tapioca & sweet beans in coconut milk

soot bull jeep

korean charcoal bbq
3136 west eighth street. between catalina and kenmore
213.387.3865
mon - sun 11a - 11p

$$: all major credit cards accepted
lunch. dinner. first come, first served

koreatown > e33

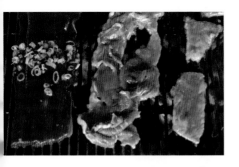

When you eat at *Soot Bull Jeep*, you get an extra added bonus: Eau de *Soot Bull Jeep*. Here's the backstory. This place is unique in the world of Korean bbq joints because their grills use coal. This creates a smoky aroma that saturates everything—from the array of eel, pork and beef cooking on your table grill to your socks. If this concerns you a bit, I can guarantee that once you start eating this food, you won't care about your post-meal scent. In fact, when people smell the Eau de SBJ on you, they may well ask why you smell so delicious.

imbibe / devour:
korean ob beer
to grill:
  kalbi short ribs
  rib eye
  squid
  eel
  spicy pork

the tasting kitchen

seasonal, northwest-inspired food

1633 abbot kinney boulevard. between venice and palms
310.392.6644 www.thetastingkitchen.com
daily 6p - close

opened in 2009. chef: casey lane
$$-$$$: all major credit cards accepted
dinner. reservations accepted

venice > **e34**

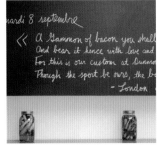

Portland, where I grew up, seems to be the city du jour these days, especially for foodies and young creative types. But it's not all wine and roses there, and some—like the entire kitchen crew at *The Tasting Kitchen*—have moved to smoggier pastures. My sister and I hung with Justin—another Portland expat—at the bar and shared P-town stories while watching him craft an array of bitters. Rumor has it that this place came together in six days, but once you taste Casey's food, you won't care if it's been open six hours or six years. It's just plain good.

imbibe / devour:
angelico cocktail
mustang cocktail
flour barrel coffee
wings with apple cider & flax seed
endive, cara cara & medjool dates salad
cod with black rice & satsuma
lamb with wild nettles, cippolinis & walnuts
tarte tatin & vanilla ice cream

umami burger

burgers for the fifth taste

850 south la brea avenue. corner of ninth
323.931.3000 www.umamiburger.com
daily 11a - 10p

opened in 2009. owner: adam fleischman
$-$$: all major credit cards accepted
lunch. dinner. first come, first served

mid-city >  e35

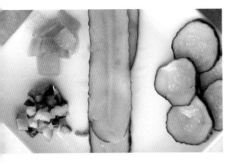

There are five different types of taste buds: sweet, salty, sour, bitter and the fifth, umami. Say what? The umami buds are the ones that recognize savory flavors, like cheeses, most meats and tomatoes—three of my favorite foods. So you would have to imagine at *Umami Burger* that the menu is a celebration of these buds. It's savory heaven. My umamis jump for joy from the first bite. And at the end of the meal, if your sweet receptors are looking for attention, don't ignore them—go ahead and have the ice cream sandwich.

imbibe / devour:
mexican coke
root beer float
hand-cut fries
house pickles
malt liquor tempura onion rings
hatch burger
umami burger
manly burger

valerie confections

chocolate and toffee

3360 west first street. between virgil and beverly
213.739.8149 www.valerieconfections.com
mon - fri 10a - 6p sat 11a - 4p

opened in 2004. owners: valerie gordon and stan weightman jr.
$: all major credit cards accepted
treats. first come, first served

silverlake > **e36**

I don't know the PR geniuses who started putting word out that chocolate is good for you, but I love them. I believe them. I trust their every word. In my world, chocolate is the new penicillin. So when I learned that *Valerie*, the lovely chocolatier whose confections I'd been admiring in various shops across the country, had its own little shop, I raced to it, knowing it was just what the doctor ordered. These pure, high-quality chocolates, toffees and truffles are exquisitely beautiful and deliciously unmatched. No marketing spin was needed to convince me of this: *Valerie* is good for you.

devour:
toffee noir
milk toffee
almond toffee treats
salt & pepper truffles
almond fleur de sel toffee
mint mendiants
hazelnut gianduja petits fours
mori ex cacao gift set

viet noodle bar

northern-style vietnamese

3133 glendale boulevard. between glenhurst and edenhurst
323.906.1575 www.vietnoodlebar.com
daily 11a - 10p

opened in 2007. owner / chef: viet tran
$-$$: cash only
lunch. dinner. first come, first served

atwater village > **e37**

I have three words for you: housemade soy milk. This menu item at *Viet Noodle Bar* might pass you by if you let it, but you would be making a whopping culinary mistake. While I could happily dine on the sandwiches and pho every day, my favorite thing here is the organic soy milk. The owner and chef, Viet, makes it by handcrushing soy beans, fermenting them, and then infusing them with herbs and spices. He is a craftsman of northern Vietnamese cuisine, where the food is simple, gently spiced and extremely seasonal. I'm just happy to know that his soy milk is in season any time of the year.

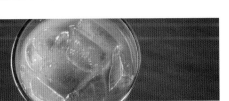

imbibe / devour:
pennywort green juice
housemade organic soymilk
vietnamese coffee
white fish noodle
lemongrass organic chicken sandwich
pho ga
jicama fresh roll
vietnamese rice noodle

village idiot

good pub with good food

7383 melrose avenue. corner of martel
323.655.3331 www.villageidiotla.com
mon - thu 11:30a - midnight fri 11:30a - 1a sat 9a - 1a sun 9a - midnight

opened in 2007. owners: charlie conrad and dean malouf
owner / chef: lindsay kennedy
$-$$: all major credit cards accepted
lunch. dinner. brunch. first come, first served

west hollywood > **e38**

At many American bars, the entertainment comes from multiple monster flat-screen TVs mounted on the walls. Patrons sit with mouths gaping, staring transfixed, unable to engage with their fellow companions. The first time I went to a gastropub in London, I marveled at the source of entertainment: the food being cooked up in plain view behind the bar and the friends people were with. What a novel idea! *The Village Idiot* gets this brilliant scheme—here, you can watch your upscale pub grub being cooked AND enjoy the company you're with, sans the boob tube. Idiots? I think not.

imbibe / devour:
craftsman heavenly heff
ballast point yellowtail pale ale
bear republic racer 5 ipa
mezze plate
steak & potato pie
fish & chips
pub burger
crispy pork belly

wurstküche

purveyor of exotic sausages

800 east third street. corner of traction
213.687.4444 www.wurstkucherestaurant.com
sun noon - midnight mon - sat 11a - midnight

opened in 2008. owners: joseph pitruzzelli and tyler wilson
$-$$: all major credit cards accepted
lunch. dinner. first come, first served

downtown >

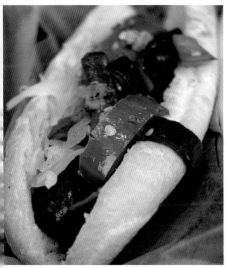

If I could conjure up any restaurant in the world to give as a gift to my husband, *Wurstküche* would be it. The appeal: good beer and exotic housemade sausages. But when we approached its doors, I suddenly worried— had I been hyping it so much that the dreaded reverse effect would happen? I angsted while we ordered and perspired while waiting for the food; even the five mustard choices did nothing to quell my anxiety. But when the rattlesnake and rabbit sausage arrived, I looked at Shawn's happy face and knew everything was a-ok. Now, why was I was worried?

imbibe / devour:
floris apple ale
schneider edel weisse
belgian fries
sausages:
    rattlesnake & rabbit with jalapeño peppers
    alligator & pork, smoked andouille sausage
    green chilies & cilantro
    apricot & ginger

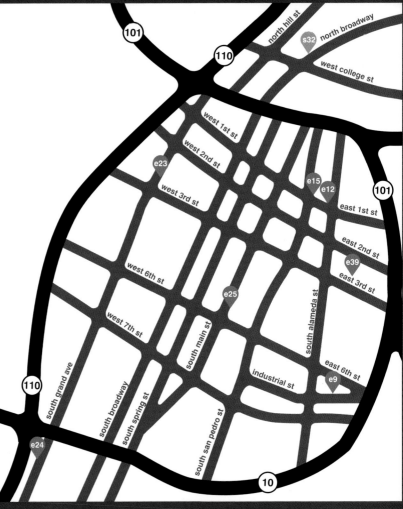

- **downtown**
- **little tokyo**

eat

e9 > church & state
e12 > daikokuya
e15 > fugetsu-do
e23 > mendocino farms
e25 > nickel diner
e24 > mo-chica
e39 > wurstküche

shop

s32 > ooga booga

NORTH

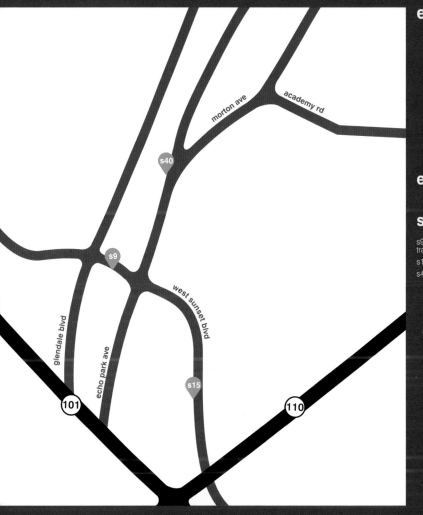

eat

shop

s9 > echo park time
traveler's mart
s15 > iko iko
s40 > tavin

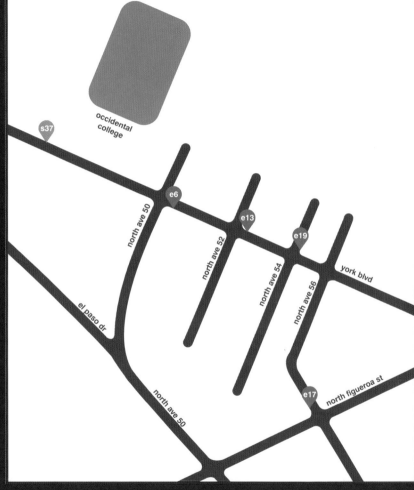

highland park

eat

e6 > café de leche
13 > el huarache azteca
e17 > good girl dinette
e19 > la estrella

shop

society of the spectacle

occidental college

s37

e6

e13

e19

north ave 50

north ave 52

north ave 54

north ave 56

york blvd

el paso dr

north ave 50

north figueroa st

e17

∧
NORTH

atwater • village silverlake

eat

e7 > canelé
e27 > palate food + win
e37 > viet noodle bar

shop

s10 > french general
s20 > lake

• silverlake

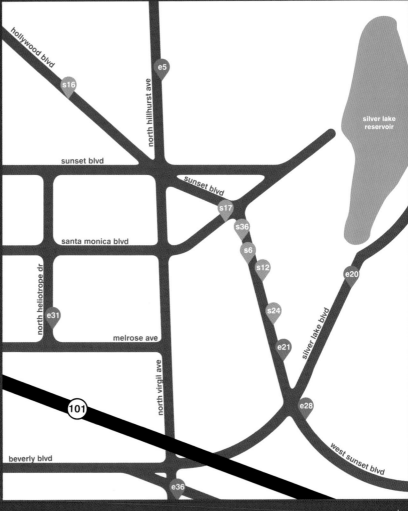

eat

e5 > best fish taco
in ensenada
e20 > lamill
e21 > lark
e28 > pho cafe
e31 > scoops
e36 > valerie confections

shop

s6 > casbah cafe and bazaar
s12 > home ec
s16 > jake
s17 > kellygreen
s24 > mas
s36 > reform school

hollywood blvd

north hillhurst ave

silver lake
reservoir

sunset blvd

sunset blvd

santa monica blvd

north heliotrope dr

melrose ave

silver lake blvd

north virgil ave

101

beverly blvd

west sunset blvd

∧
NORTH

s16
e5
s17
s36
s6
s12
e20
e31
s24
e21
e28
e36

hollywood •
west •
hollywood

eat

e14 > food + lab
e38 > village idiot

shop

s7 > church
s8 > creatures of comfort
s13 > house on genesee
s23 > lost and found stores

midcity:
west

eat

e2 > animal
e18 > joan's on 3rd
e22 > loteria grill

shop

s18 > king's beads, inc.
s19 > krislyn design
s28 > new stone age
s29 > noodle stories
s31 > ok
s33 > plastica
s38 > south willard
s44 > traveler's bookcase
s45 > zelen

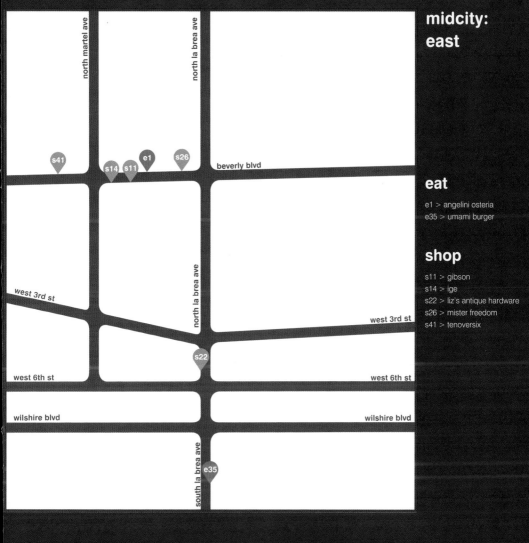

midcity:
east

eat

e1 > angelini osteria
e35 > umami burger

shop

s11 > gibson
s14 > ige
s22 > liz's antique hardware
s26 > mister freedom
s41 > tenoversix

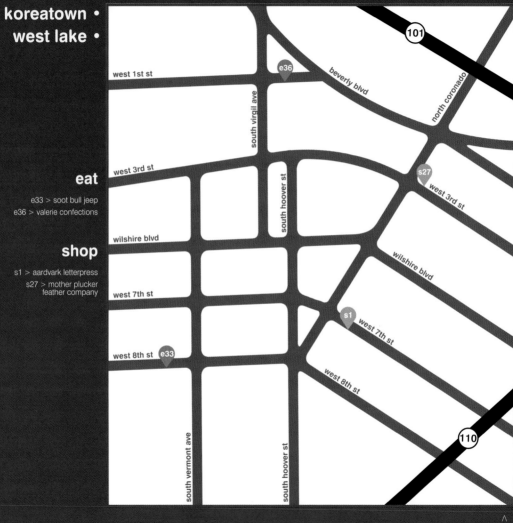

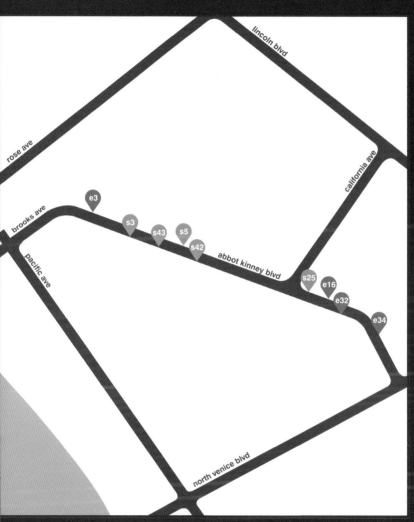

venice •

eat

e3 > axe
e16 > gjelina
e32 > shima
e34 > the tasting kitchen

shop

s3 > bazar
s5 > bountiful
s25 > milkmade
s42 > tortoise
s43 > tortoise general store

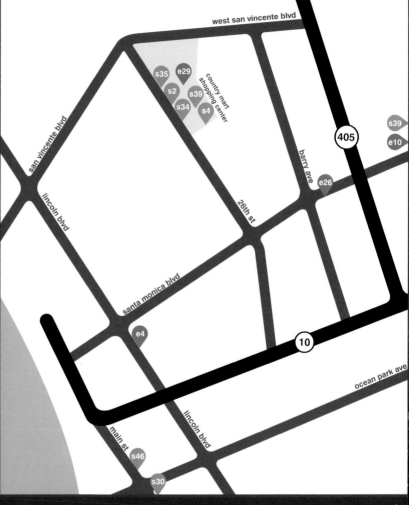

• santa monica brentwood

eat

e4 > bay cities
e10 > clementine
e26 > nook bistro
e29 > reddi-chick

shop

s2 > apartment number 9
s4 > botany
s30 > obsolete
(off the map)
s34 > poppy store
s35 > post 26
s39 > sugar paper
(2nd location)
s39 > sugar paper
(1st location off map)
s46 > zenbunni

NORTH

notes

aardvark letterpress

classic, custom letterpress shop
2500 west seventh street. corner of carondelet
213.388.2271 www.aardvarkletterpress.com
mon - fri 10a - 6p sat 10a - 2p

opened in 1968. owners: brooks and cary ocon
all major credit cards accepted
custom orders only

downtown >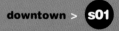

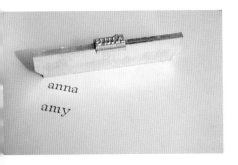

The day I visited *Aardvark Letterpress* was perhaps my favorite day of work I've ever had. I showed up unannounced with my sister, Amy. The incredibly gracious Brooks without hesitation proceeded to give us an extensive guided tour. Amy and I have longed for years to start our own letterpress business, so we were peeling our jaws from the ground drooling over the Heidelberg press in action. Though sadly there's not a retail side to this operation, I will absolutely have *Aardvark* do some cards or invites for me. As for my sister, she's going to try to wrangle an apprenticeship here.

covet:
anything that is printed here, like:
  invitations
  note cards
  personal stationery
  business cards

apartment number 9

a store for men

225 26th street. in the brentwood country mart
310.394.9440 www.apartmentnumber9.com
mon - sat 10 - 6p sun noon - 5p

opened in 2004. owners: sarah and amy blessing
all major credit cards accepted

brentwood >  **s02**

With two big sisters, I struggle with Little Sister Syndrome. For the past nine years, I've had a multitude of friends, acquaintances—heck even family—ask me, "How's your store doing?" Despite earning a master's in journalism and securing a rather interesting job of my own, everyone is fascinated with *Apartment Number 9*. I'm beginning to realize that I don't mind being mistaken for an owner, and next time someone asks me how "my" store is, I'm going to reply, "Fantastic. Thanks for asking." I'll happily bask in a little of the praise.

covet:
bbb handknit alpaca / cashmere hats
rag & bone coats
jack spade cashmere
vintage cufflinks
band of outsiders ties
unis sweaters
pantherella cashmere socks

bazar

unusual finds, old and new
1108c abbot kinney boulevard. between westminster and san juan
310.314.2101
wed - sun noon - 6p

opened in 1998. owner: tina wakino
visa. mc

venice > s03

Here's some definitions for a bazaar. 1. A market consisting of a street lined with shops and stalls, especially in the Orient or Middle East. 2. A shop in which miscellaneous articles are sold. 3. An outstanding place in Venice that encompasses the first two meanings of the word. Though this modern *Bazar* is tucked on the Abbot Kinney strip, you could imagine once inside that you were far, far away from Southern California. And like the busy souks of Morrocco or Cairo, this street on a weekend demands some respite which you can find inside the calmness of this intriguing spot.

covet:
vintage linens
mister freedom denim
japanese street signs
felt rocks
woven bags
antique boards with arabic script
vintage furniture
pillows & throws

botany

desirable florals
225 26th street. in the brentwood country mart
310.394.0358 www.botanyflowers.com
mon - sat 10a - 6p sun 11a - 5p

opened in 2009. owners: stacie rubaum and stephanie schur
all major credit cards accepted
custom orders / design. events

brentwood > **s04**

K: I see the email from Anna; it seems urgent. It goes something like this: "Kaie. There's a new florist that's just opened in the Country Mart. You NEED to go check it out." And so, I hopped in my rented Dodge Caravan and careened down PCH to *Botany* (12 minutes from Malibu to Brentwood, not bad!). And yes Anna, your sources had it right. *Botany* is gorgeous. My first sight of this little space at the back of the Mart was of a black wall that seemed to be sprouting flowers. Smile. And then talking to the effervescent Stacie made me want to have her fill my world with blooms.

covet:
gorgeous arrangements
cut flowers
succulents
terrariums
citrus trees
beekman 1802 soaps
haws watering can
d. landreth seeds

107

bountiful

pretty things for a pretty home
1335 abbot kinney boulevard. between santa clara and california
310.450.3620 www.bountifulhome.com
tue - sat 9a - 5p

opened in 1996. owner: sue balmforth
visa. mc

venice >

I used to go to Florida every year for spring break with my family. We stayed at my grandparents' place where we would spend hours on the white beach looking for seashells. My grandmother had an incredible eye; she could find the rarest, most beautiful shells, and her collection was exquisite. The big bins of shells at *Bountiful* make me think of her and her finds. While I will never have her skill in seeking, and my trips to Florida have become rare, I can always come to this sun-bleached shop and fill bags of seashells to take home with me, in case I need a bit of the sea and Gammy's memory.

covet:
shells, shells & more shells!
cake stand collection
alabaster lamps
chandeliers
vintage armoires
cote bastide bath products
maria evora soaps

casbah café and bazaar

moroccan bazaar

3900 west sunset boulevard. corner of hyperion
323.664.7000 www.casbahcafe.com
sun - thu 8a - 10p fri - sat 8a - 11p

all major credit cards accepted

silverlake > s06

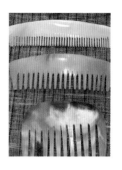

On the other side of the globe, things are different: different temperatures, different modes of transportation, different neighborhood cafés. But step into *Casbah Café* and you'll feel like you've covered the distance in no time flat. Suddenly you're in a café in the middle of Morocco, Algeria, Egypt or Turkey. Even better, this café contains a bazaar, offering up silk wraps, leather sandals, tortoise shell combs and all variety of imported treasures, many of them custom made just for this store. All this, and you've only traveled the distance from your car to *Casbah*.

covet:
camel leather shoes
stitched silk cloths
embroidered tunics
woven & beaded necklaces
hair combs
printed tablecloths
colorful scarves
hand-stitched leather journals

church

statement-making clothing, jewelry and accessories

7277 santa monica boulevard. corner of greenacre
323.876.8887 www.churchboutique.com
mon - fri 10a - 7p sat 11a - 7p

opened in 2009. owners: david malvaney and rodney burns
all major credit cards accepted

west hollywood > s07

Growing up, my dad took me to just about every variety of church you could imagine: Greek Orthodox, Southern Baptist, Maranatha—even coffeehouse varieties that didn't meet in an actual church. It was quite the education. But I've never been to a church like this *Church*. I saw immediately why people worship here. It's like David and Rodney have created a new kind of religion, showing fresh perspectives from the fashion world. I felt my horizons opening to exciting new worlds. This *Church* is one I could really get excited about.

covet:
jennifer mary
raquel allegra
coquette
liana reid
endovanera
little doe
cerre
riser goodwin

creatures of comfort

both indie and established women's clothing

7971 melrose avenue. between edinburgh and hayworth
323.655.7855 www.creaturesofcomfort.us
mon - sat 11a - 7p sun noon - 6p

opened in 2005. owner: jade lai
all major credit cards accepted
online shopping

west hollywood > **s08**

I am a creature of comfort. When I wake up on a Saturday morning and I'm hanging around the house, I tend to pull on a pair of sweats or leggings and a soft t-shirt rather than a pair of skinny jeans and a structured shirt. Even when I venture outside the house, an occasion when style comes first, comfort is a close second. This is why I'm fond of *Creatures of Comfort*. Style is at the forefront here with some very sharp brands, but this goes hand-in-hand with everything being extremely wearable. I'm so comfortable in this store, I wish I never had to leave.

covet:
manu jewelry
acne
etoile isabel marant
vpl underwear
map tote bags
zero maria cornejo
apc
united bamboo

115

echo park time traveler's mart

everything you need for time travel
1714 west sunset boulevard. between lemoyne and logan
213.413.3388 www.826la.org
mon - fri noon - 8p sat - sun noon - 6p

opened in 2008
all major credit cards accepted
online shopping. writing classes at 826

echo park > **s09**

If you could time travel, where would you go? Would you watch your mom as a coed in college? Observe the moment electricity was discovered? Transport to Vienna to ogle Beethoven as a young master? Well, you best start thinking about your chosen time, because *Echo Park Time Travel Mart* has the tools you need to be on your way. Okay, well, it's just all play, but it's play that is front to a real activity: the *826LA* writing program for kids. So while this might not be Marty McFly's DeLorean, there's much fun to be had here while contributing to some great kids' futures.

covet:
time traveler brand leeches
donuts from 1985
evolutions! opposable thumbs
moustaches
caveman candy
auntie nantucket's cold-pressed whale oil
tkbrand double chubble
caveman flint

french general

vintage fabrics, notions and papers

2009 riverside drive. off of the glendale and golden state freeways
323.668.0488 www.frenchgeneral.com
mon 11a - 4p

opened in 1999. owner: kaari meng
all major credit cards accepted
online shopping. workshops. special events

silverlake > **s10**

My sisters and I recently started a craft blog (wanton self-promotion here: bbbcraft.blogspot.com). It's mostly about sharing the various doodads and whatnots we like to make. I'll admit our collective dream is to someday be full-time crafters. In other words, we are totally jealous of Kaari. Her store, *French General*, is soooo pretty, filled with fabrics and notions and vintage papers that would make any crafter swoon deeply. Her books and kits are hugely inspirational for us crafties. And if crafting isn't your thing, no worries—there's plenty here for you as well. *French General*, I've got a crush on you.

covet:
sewing charm bracelet kit
rouenneries fabric collection
lavender travel pillows
grain sack bags
vintage linen sheets
beads & buttons
vintage papers
handmade soirees by kaari meng

gibson

both art and interiors
7350 beverly boulevard. corner of fuller
323.934.4248 www.garygibson.com
mon - fri 9a - 6p sat 11a - 5p

opened in 2002. owner: gary gibson
all major credit cards accepted

mid-city > s11

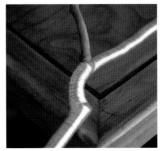

It's hard for me to really get seduced by a white-walled, starkly lit, sterile art gallery. Though the art on the walls might be enticing, I find the experience too disconnected from how the art might look in my home. At *Gibson*, artwork mingles with found objects, vintage furniture and a variety of unexpected items. Aha! This is what I'm talking about. Here I can get the sense of how pieces would work in my world. I liked *Gibson* so much, I wondered if I could move in. Seems that's not an option, but I can use the design services of the folks here to help me recreate my own *Gibson* feel at home.

covet:
klairat brown ceramics
jim gentry
michael koch
nancy levy
alissa warshaw
michael shemchuk
donald robson

home ec

craft supplies and kits
3815 west sunset boulevard. between hyperion and lucile
323.906.8826 www.homeecshop.com
tue - fri noon - 7p sat - sun 11a - 7p

opened in 2009. owner: jenny ryan
visa. mc
online shopping. workshops. special events

silverlake > **s12**

Do they still teach home ec in school? I took it in 7th grade and got to sew a goofy looking animal pillow and bake some sticky buns—this was school at its most fun. This *Home Ec* is a little more refined, as it's filled with cool goods from expert crafters who were the types in junior high who excelled with the sewing machine and have just gotten more talented over time. If you are the type who might sew your thumbs together, not to worry, you can also come here to take classes from the experts or to just buy some really cool stuff.

covet:
wool roving in many colors
amy butler patterns
wooden gift tags
kits, kits & more kits!
knitting, crochet & felting tools
wallpaper projects
sublime stitching
handmade pincushions

house on genesee

a family-run store, gallery, cafe and more

1300 north genesee. corner of fountain
323.845.9821 www.houseongenesee.com
tue - sat 11a - 7p sun noon - 6p

opened in 2009. owners: alex, gabriela and tere artigas
visa. mc
special events. lunch by appointment

west hollywood > s13

You will leave *House on Genesee* with two emotions. The first will be complete jaw-dropping awe. The second will be jealousy that you aren't the fourth Artigas sibling. This immensely talented family has created a house that is not a home, but a store, a place to eatand a studio. Alex crafts the furniture, Gabriela the jewelry and Tere the fresh juice you will enjoy in respite in the peaceful backyard. Everything you might desire is in this magical house. Everything, that is, except the adoption papers for that would make you an adjunct Artigas family member.

covet:
artless furniture
gabriela artigas jewelry
bang buro
farm tactics
zan zan eyewear
taller flora by carla fernandez
odyn vovk
esquivel

ige

artful lifestyle store
7382 beverly boulevard. between martel and fuller
323.939.2788 www.igedesign.com
mon - sat 11a - 6p

opened in 2003. owner: helene ige
all major credit cards accepted
online shopping

mid-city > **s14**

I just read a newspaper story about a recall of children's jewelry made with a toxic and carcinogenic metal. Yikes, how far removed have we become from the people and places that make our goods, that this sort of thing happens?! At *Ige*, you are barely one step removed. Witness Helene who works at the back of her store, putting together her amazing mobiles. And most other objects sold here are made my hand—by real people, not by real big factories. Everything here feels like an individual work of art. And nontoxic art at that.

covet:
ige:
  canvas calendar
  laser-cut mobiles
  pillows
patch nyc mushrooms
k studio pouches & books
dbo home ceramics
sandy vohr's leather zoo

iko iko

thematic hi-craft
1298 sunset boulevard. corner of innes
323.719.1079 www.ikoikospace.com
tue - sat 1 - 7p sun 1 - 5p

opened in 2009. owner: kristin dickson
all major credit cards accepted
online shopping

echo park > **s15**

K: As any of the *eat.shop* authors will tell you, when writing these tomes we often find ourselves using the same words to describe items or places. Sure we can pull out the thesaurus and dig around, but usually this yields pretty bland results. For awhile now I've been looking for the perfect term to describe small-batch, artist-based designs and then Kristin at *Iko Iko* handed the term to me on a platter: hi-craft. Yes, yes, YES! Of course she would have coined this because her ever-evolving space (her store theme changes every six weeks or so) is a mecca of hi-kraft. All hail, Kristin.

covet:
rowena sartin (the house line)
hannah keefe soldered jewelry
waka waka furniture & objects
ashley helvey felted wool necklaces
mark borthwick polaroids
vintage design books
jen smith canning series
casa bruno magazine

jake

vintage styles for men
4644 hollywood boulevard. between vermont and hillhurst
323.662.5253 www.jakevintage.com
tue - sat noon - 7p sun noon - 5p

opened in 2007. owner: jonathan kanarek
all major credit cards accepted

los feliz > **s16**

I often see stores when I'm researching a city that seem as though someone had the off-the-cuff thought, "How cool would it be to own a store?" Then set up shop in a half-baked way, with slat walls, plastic hangers and no specific point of view. Imagine this, then picture the opposite, and you have *Jake*. There couldn't be a more carefully conceived, edited, merchandised and displayed store than this. Jonathan long dreamed of creating this store with its lounge-cum-dressing-room vibe. Men, if vintage wear from the '40s - '60s is your bag, then *Jake* is your place.

covet:
vintage:
  suits
  ties
  sport coats
  trousers
  cuff links
  plaid shirts
  hats

131

kellygreen

goods for a green life
4008 santa monica boulevard. at sunset
323.481.4193 www.kellygreenhome.com
tue - sun 11a - 7p

opened in 2007. owner: kelly van patter
all major credit cards accepted
design services

silverlake > **s17**

Having only one job is soooo last decade. Take it from Kelly, who runs her own interior design company and this incredible, all-things-green shop. More and more people I know are diversifying—out of necessity, boredom or just plain interest—and creating multiple careers for themselves. If a second or third career isn't in the works for you this year, why not take your new year's resolutions one step at a time and go green? The first stop; *Kellygreen*, of course, where there are enough products, books and ideas to get you started on the right path.

covet:
cedar shoe fresh inserts
every book about green living you'll ever need
reusable dry cleaner hanging bags
spools of twine
staple-less stapler
harry barker hemp dog toys
cate & levi handmade kids' toys
eco lunch sacks

kings beads, inc.

jam-packed bead shop
309 north kings road. corner of beverly
323.782.0209 www.kingsbeadsla.com
mon - fri 10a - 6p sat - sun 11a - 7p

visa. mc

mid-city >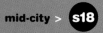

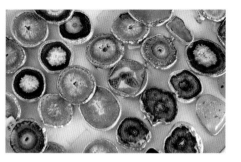

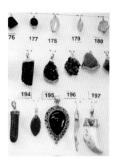

Just because L.A. is a mecca for creative industries, doesn't mean that creativity is always obvious here. It can get hidden behind the glossy facades of fancy malls, swanky rides and the abundance of plastic surgery (though this can get quite creative). *Kings Beads* is a creative harbor for jewelers, both amateur and professional. It's stocked from floor to ceiling (no joke—there are beads touching the floor that hang all the way from the ceiling) with gems, chains, findings, cords, etc. of every shape, color and size. Only a creative sort of town could support such an amazing gem of a shop.

covet:
silver & gold chains
flat silver discs
gold filigree leaves
turquoise
cord, twine & thread
semi-precious faceted beads
agate rings
coral beads

krislyn design

floral couture

8216 west third street. between sweetzer and la jolla
323.692.7862 www.krislyndesign.com
mon - fri 10a - 5p

opened in 2005. owners: krislyn komarov
all major credit cards accepted
online shopping. custom orders. classes

mid-city >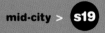

I have seen a zillion stores all over this country. After awhile they tend to blur together, and I often can't remember what I saw where, or in which city. *Krislyn Design* is not one of those places. It is a place that will remain etched deeply in my memory. A place where the concept of floral seems shockingly new, and the talent behind it is almost obscene. I find *Krislyn* hard to categorize, impossible to copy and sure to impress. Whether or not you're in the market for a cloud tree or a porcelain mushroom, please please please, don't miss out on this magical place.

covet:
white japanese dream
obsidian wind chime
mica mobile
brass pod candlesticks
balsa flower pod
driftwood candelabra
balsa flower centerpiece
barnacle vase

lake

lovely women's boutique
2910 rowena avenue. between hyperion and glendale
323.664.6522 www.lakeboutique.com
sun - mon noon - 6p tue - fri noon - 7p sat 11a - 7p

opened in 2007. owner: melissa lovoy
all major credit cards accepted

silverlake > 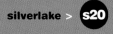 **s20**

There are some stores you want to shop in and others you want to relocate to. *Lake* is the latter as it seems so much more economical and logical to settle in here instead of moving all of these things into my home. What's so special about this clothing/apothecary/lifestyle store? I find that all of the well thought out components of a comfortable, beautiful life are here, including some incredibly comfy leather chairs. If Melissa won't let me move in, maybe I'll just slip on some of the clothing and position myself on the chair as a living mannequin and make myself useful.

covet:
elizabeth & james
fleur wood
inhabit
james perse
nili lotan
rag & bone
melissa joy manning
mike & chris

linus bikes

modern classic city bikes
1413 1/2 abbot kinney boulevard. between california and milwood
310.857.7777 www.linusbike.com
daily 11a - 7p

opened in 2009. owners: adam mcdermott and chad kushner
all major credit cards accepted

venice >

I probably walked by the attractive, shiny bikes lined up along Abbot Kinney in front of *Milkmade* maybe five or six times before I realized that they were part of an outdoor showroom of sorts for the locally made *Linus Bikes*. Walk down the alley and there you'll find a small store where you can further admire an array of bikes, smartly designed bike bags and accessories and get a chance to meet the owners and bikemakers. I've been on the lookout for a classic city bike for a couple of years now, and a cream colored *Linus* bike with all the accoutrements is now at the top of my wish list.

covet:
bikes:
  roadster classic
  roadster sport
  dutchi
  mixte
baskets
bags

liz's antique hardware

vintage and reproduction hardware
453 south la brea avenue. between fourth and sixth
323.939.4403 www.lahardware.com / www.theloftatlizs.com
mon - sat 10a - 6p

opened in 1988. owner: liz gordon
all major credit cards accepted
online shopping

mid-city >

The house I grew up in is a turn-of-the-century Tudor. Living in a place with leaded glass windows and vintage plumbing meant numerous trips to big old hardware stores that specialized in vintage fittings. So even though I might have thought these trips were pretty ho-hum as a child, I now love visiting places like *Liz's Antique Hardware* with its well-loved doorknobs and perfectly well-worn trims. Even if your SoCal home is filled with shiny and modern things, *Liz's* will help you inject it with a bit of brassy patina and vintage glamour.

covet:
antique hardware:
  light fixtures
  doorknobs
  doors
  bathroom fixtures
  keyholes
  door trim
  doorplates

lost and found stores

collection of stores for women, men and children
6314 - 6324 yucca street. between ivar and vine
323.856.5872
mon - sat 10a - 6p

opened in 1999. owner: jamie rosenthal
visa. mc

hollywood >

It's possible that one day we'll wake up, and Jamie will have taken over L.A. As we speak, her little empire of *Lost and Found* is ever growing on Yucca Street with a gallery, a men's store and her quintessential women's and children's outposts. Walking into any of these places feels like being on the other side of the wardrobe door, and though you may feel as if you've landed in a magical land, you will still be firmly planted in Jamie's world. I apologize for having only five meager pictures to illustrate how fantastic this world is. This just means you'll just have to get yourself here posthaste.

covet:
feal mor
local
repetto
aris geldis
lucky fish
missoni home
maria la rosa
sydney's pottery

mas

men's and women's contemporary clothing

3511 1/2 sunset boulevard. between maltman and golden gate
323.663.3112 www.masboutique.com
tue - fri noon - 8p sat 11a - 7p sun noon - 5p

opened in 2007. owner: shanon benedetti
all major credit cards accepted
online shopping

silverlake >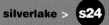

I'm generally of the "less-is-more" mindset when it comes to most things. I tend to want fewer things, less color, less ornament, fewer accessories. Except when I come to *Mas*, where I want more, more, more! Why suddenly this overwhelming desire? Simple. *Mas* is filled with the type of clothing I want to wear: strong statement pieces mixed with casual basics. And when I find a place that speaks my language the way this place does, I want to take full advantage of the opportunity. *Una mas*!

---

covet:
maggie ward sueded silk sweatpants
rachel comey smocked dress
crispin & basilio tunic top
geren ford snap-front coat
kenneth jay lane elephant bracelet
shipley & halmos dress
alexander wang tank dress
toms shoes

milkmade

stylish shop for guys and girls

1413 abbot kinney boulevard. between california and milwood
310.581.8890 www.shop.milkmade.eu
tue - sat 11a - 7p sun noon - 6p

opened in 2008. owner: brian j. lee
all major credit cards accepted
online shopping

venice > **s25**

It's generally a good thing that my growing belly has forced some restraint when it comes to shopping while I'm working on these books. But when I entered *Milkmade*, I was immediately bummed about the limitations brought on by my quickly expanding baby girth, i.e. a stretchy waistband is imperative. This is a store with beautifully tailored clothing with intricate details that show off a figure—clothing that is quite the opposite of the shapeless tents I'm wearing right now. Ahhh *Milkmade*, I will return to you. Just as soon as I'm out of my pull-up pants.

covet:
harvey faircloth
hoss jewelry
sessun sweaters & jackets
trovata everything
the vael project boots
le labo candles
apolis activism
dunderdon

mister freedom

vintage clothing, shoes and accessories
7161 beverly boulevard. between formosa and detroit
323.653.2014 www.misterfreedom.com
daily noon - 7p

opened in 1990. owner: christophe loiron
all major credit cards accepted

mid-city > **s26**

I often feel like there are fewer than six degrees of separation between the businesses that appear in these books. In this case, it was three degrees: *Lost and Found* headed me to *Bazar* where I was aimed to *Mister Freedom*. It's like playing connect the dots, with this final dot making me feel like I'd wandered onto the set of M*A*S*H*. *Mister Freedom* is half filled with vintage army boots, jeans, t's and military memorabilia. The other half is all about the in-house line of Japanese selvedge denim. Now I'm going to try to connect Kevin Bacon and Alan Alda in six steps.

covet:
mister freedom originals:
  selvedge denim
  jackets
  t's
vintage:
  sweatshirts
  jeans
  boots

mother plucker feather company

the name says it all

2511 west third street. between coronado and carondelet
213.637.0411 www.motherplucker.com
mon - fri 10a - 6p

opened in the early 1970s. owner: william zelowitz
all major credit cards accepted

These days when people open a business, they tend to name it something minimalistic and understated. In Willy's case, he could have easily named his spot something like *Plume* and called it a day. But he had a bit of fun and called it *Mother Plucker*. Ha! Love it, as this place is the mother lode of plucked plumes. Willy knows his s*#! and whether you're in the market for pheasant, ostrich, or some other exotic variety of feather, he's got it. And even if you have no use for this type of decoration, it's well worth a trip here to see all this plumage on display.

covet:
feathers:
  guinea hen, large eye
  ring neck pheasant, almond
  pheasant tail/red tip
  lady amherst tail
  male ostrich plume
  boas & more

new stone age

glorious gifts

8407 west third street. between croft and orlando
323.658.5969 www.newstoneagela.com
mon - sat 11a - 6p sun noon - 5p

opened in 1982. owner: fran ayres
visa. mc

mid-city > **s28**

My family members are competitive gift givers. Over the years it's almost developed into an extreme sport (maybe ESPN will devote a channel to it): who finds unique things, who wraps the most creatively, who follows a theme the best. So come birthdays and holidays, the pressure is on. With *New Stone Age* as my secret weapon, I'm now calm as the proverbial cucumber. Just about everything in this store is bound to impress my picky clan, and I'm pretty certain that these treasures are going to help win me the gold medal of gift giving.

covet:
letter balls
a veritable emporium of jewelry!
bird whistles
ceramic keys
vintage metallic thread
emporium glass glitter
absinthe sucre
goody grams animal shot glasses

noodle stories

fashion-forward women's store
8323 west third street. between flores and sweetzer
323.651.1782 www.noodlestories.com
mon - sat 10 - 6p sun noon - 5p

opened in 1995. owner: caryl kim
all major credit cards accepted

mid-city > **s29**

Who is it that came up with the rules for dressing, and why do we blindly follow ones like the silly "No white linen after Labor Day?" Who knows. So thank goodness there's a place like *Noodle Stories*—where they celebrate breaking the rules and being fashion nonconformists. This is where you can find shoes that don't necessarily match perfectly and clothes that playfully disregard symmetry. If having fun with fashion and being an individualist appeals to your sharp and savvy noodle, then *Noodle Stories* is the place for you.

covet:
viktor & rolf
tao
martin margiela
junya watanabe
comme des garçons
antipast
y's by yohji yamamoto
hache

obsolete

industrial and found objects from the past

222 main street. between marine and rose
310.399.0024 www.obsoleteinc.com
mon, wed - sun 11a - 6p

opened in 2000. owner: ray azoulay
all major credit cards accepted

venice >

When her son complained of being bored, *Mad Men's* Betty Draper retorted, "Boring people are bored; go bang your head against a wall." My real-world advice for those afflicted with ennui? "Boring people are bored; go to *Obsolete*." It's not possible for boredom to exist here. The moment you set foot into this amazing place, you'll feel as though you've entered another realm of the universe. Though many of the eclectic array of objects may have come from obsolete eras, new life has come to them when co-mingled with modern, slighty macabre artwork. This *Obsolete* is the antithesis of over.

covet:
vintage:
   sculpture / side table with cast-iron base
   question-mark industrial light
   nickel-plated utility mirror
   french primitive wooden horse toy
tom haney
anne siems
ethan murrow

ok

home goods and personal accessories
8303 west third street. corner of sweetzer
323.653.3501 www.okthestore.com
mon - sat 11a - 6:30p sun noon - 6p

opened in 1999. owner: larry schaffer
all major credit cards accepted
online shopping. registries

mid-city > s31

You will find that a lot modern lifestyle stores (also called urban tchotchke stores) stock a large selection of silly fluff—i.e., goofily designed objects with no useful purpose other than to clutter up one's life. *OK* is not one of said stores. You will find absolutely no fluff here. This is a store where every item has a purpose. Each of these carefully chosen objects is well vetted by the knowledgeable and no-nonsense Larry who has a sharp eye for finding the quality goods you want in your home. Fun, ok. Fluff, not ok.

covet:
heath ceramics
noguchi lamp
vintage phones
riedel glassware
anne ricketts bronze sculptures
enzo mari perpetual calendar
imco lighter
riviera baby press rollerball pen

ooga booga

art, printed matter, jewelry, posters and more
943 north broadway #203. between lei min way and gin ling way
213.617.1105 www.oogaboogastore.com
tue - sat noon - 7p   sun noon - 5p

opened in 2004. owner: wendy yao
all major credit cards accepted

chinatown > **s32**

As the modern world expands with millions of cool new products, tools and technologies to make day-to-day living faster and easier, it's obvious that we are gaining efficiency. Sadly, this also means we are moving away from creating with our hands. But never fear as *Ooga Booga* is here. This is a place that celebrates the intimate, the thoughtful and the creative. This is a place where the art of creating physical things hasn't been overshadowed by the world of mass manufacturing or electronics. Now, if you'll excuse me, I'm going to send a quick tweet about this spot.

covet:
mason cooley
sarah shapiro
mika miko
mended veil
andrew jeffrey
violet hopkins
slow and steady wins the race
lucy mckenzie

163

plastica

colorful, functional objects

8405 west third street. between orlando and croft
323.655.1051 www.plasticashop.com
mon - sat 11a - 6p sun noon - 5p

opened in 2000. owner: carla denker
all major credit cards accepted
online shopping

mid-city > **s33**

I have one word for you: *Plastica*. Maybe if this had been the advice young Benjamin Braddock had been given at his graduation party, he might not have gotten seduced by Mrs. Robinson. No doubt this store could lure in anyone, old and young alike, curing those who think shopping is boring. I know this is a big claim for a simple store, but check out *Plastica's* punchy-colored array of playfully functional, internationally-sourced items and you'll agree. Remember, when giving useful tips, *Plastica* should be at the top of your list.

covet:
bento boxes
modkat litter box
whitelines perfect bound notebook
lamy safari pen & pencil
france matchbook postcards
bierfilzl wool coasters
stelton vacuum jug
nimikko slippers

poppy store

luxe essentials for kids

225 26th street. in the brentwood country mart
310.260.0002 www.poppystores.com
mon - sat 11a - 6p sun noon - 6p

opened in 2008. owners: heather whitney and jenny belushi
all major credit cards accepted
online shopping

brentwood >

The problem with most children's stores is this: they're either too adult-oriented or too kid-oriented. The adult-style kids' stores are so stuffy the kids don't know if they're in a store or the doctor's office. Then there are the kid-style, I-want-this-now-or-I'm-throwing-a-massive-tantrum stores filled with cheap plastic items that your child will tire of in an hour. *Poppy Store*, thankfully, is neither. They have cool clothing and toys that moms from Echo Park to Santa Monica will love and glass jars filled with curiosities that kids will be glued to. Happiness for all.

covet:
maloup clothing
makié clothing
superga sneakers
serena & lily market sling
sophie giraffe
vilac wooden toys
lacoste headbands
hunter wellies

post 26

stylish shop for women

225 26th street. in the brentwood country mart
310.451.0950 www.post26.com
mon - sat 10a - 6p sun noon - 4p

opened in 2006. owners: jeannine braden and kay sides
all major credit cards accepted

brentwood > **s35**

Jeannine is someone's best friend. I'm insanely jealous of whoever this person is because Jeannine is the best friend we all want: fashionable, witty and able to think outside the box—just like her store *Post 26*. This place is packed, and I mean PACKED, with vintage shoes, new designs, old designs, refurbished jewelry, etc. You want her as a best friend to lend you a pair of shoes for a first date or to have that last perfect accessory on the day of your wedding. You'll want her for every style crisis and celebration. For now, just shop at her store. It's the next best thing to having Jeannine as your best friend.

covet:
alexander wang
3.1 phillip lim
anya hindmarch
rick owens lillies
see by chloe
k jacques shoes
anna sui
88 by bing bang

reform school

things from indie crafters and artists

3902 sunset boulevard. between hyperion and sanborn
323.906.8660 www.reformschoolrules.com
mon - fri noon - 7p sat 11a - 7p sun 11a - 6p

opened in 2005. owners: tootie maldonado and billie lopez
all major credit cards accepted
online shopping

silverlake >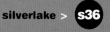

Ever since I was in grad school for journalism, I've dreamed of being the editor-in-chief at a craft magazine. The first thing I would do at the helm of this fantasy mag would be to source all of my talent and ideas from the brilliant creatives whose goods can be found at *Reform School.* This is a place where everything on display has been rethought and reformed for the new millennium. Where smart, thoughtful and wicked creative crafting is a long way away from grandma's knit tea cozies and macramé doilies. Though I'm long done with school, I'm just getting started at *Reform School.*

covet:
kg + ab porcelain mixed nuts
alyssa ettinger ceramic knit coaster set
k studio pillows
hillery sproatt mobile
magno wooden radio
japanese masking tape
camera obscura kit
wooden button set

society of the spectacle

groovy eyeware

4563 york boulevard. between avenue 46 and eagle rock
323.255.4300 www.societyspectacle.com
mon - fri 11a - 7p sat 10a - 6p sun noon - 5p

opened in 2007. owners: katie and amy o'connell
all major credit cards accepted

highland park >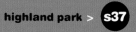

You don't need to be a genius to figure out this is a town of sunglasses. Yes, there is plenty of sun here to warrant the use of protective eyeware—but this is also a place where folks wear sunglasses at midnight to (try and) look cool. Whatever the reason you wear them, the place to buy sunglasses and just plain old glasses is *Society of the Spectacle*. The sisters behind *S of the S* have 30 years experience in the sunglasses industry, so they know their stuff. Plus, I love that many of the lines they stock are California-based, so you're getting a truly authentic Golden State experience here.

covet:
sunglasses & glasses:
  ray ban
  salt
  oliver peoples
  l.a. eyewear
  kaenon
  vintage

south willard

a soothing, smart men's store
8038 west third street. between crescent heights and edinburgh
323.653.6153 www.southwillard.com
mon - sat noon - 6p sun noon - 5p

opened in 2004. owners: ryan conder and danielle kays
all major credit cards accepted
online shopping

mid-city > **s38**

Do you find these days that being calm is a bit tough? Most people I know are having to double-up on the Bikram yoga to help keep the stress at bay. I have a different method, which is to visit *South Willard*. Neutral and primary colored men's clothing and accessories is the story here, with everything carefully hung, placed and stacked in moderation—with attention to straight lines and even spacing. Ahhh, I'm soothed just thinking about it. Men, if you don't want thumping music blasting away while you shop or duuuuuudes helping you find your wardrobe, this is your spot.

covet:
stephan schneider
vibram sandals for south willard
band of outsiders ties
postal co card cases
dries van noten
mhl. shirts
margaret howell
quody for south willard

sugar paper

custom letterpress studio and paper goods shop
sm: 1749 ensley avenue. between eastborne and santa monica
bw: 225 26th street. in the brentwood country mart
310.277.7804 www.sugarpaper.com
mon - fri 10a - 6p sat 10a - 5p sun 10a - 5p

opened in 2003. owners: chelsea shukov and jamie grobecker
all major credit cards accepted
online shopping. custom orders

century city / brentwood > s39

Yes, Virginia, there are people who still write letters. Take for example, my friend Katie, who writes such eloquent thank you notes, I'm tempted to frame them. My thank yous pale in comparison with Katie's, but I do love to send and receive beautiful cards, and one of the best places to find gorgeous goods is at *Sugar Paper*. From custom letterpress to their own prettier-than-pretty line of paper goods to a carefully picked assortment of other letterpressed delights—the message you send on something from here will be memorable, whether you're able to express it in words or by your choice of card.

covet:
sugar paper:
  audrey desk calendar
  recipe box
  alphabet coasters
  market list
oh joy note pads
hammerpress calendars
beautiful wrapping papers

tavin

vintage boutique
1543 echo park avenue. between glaston and morton
213.482.5832 www.lifebytavin.com
tue - sun noon - 7p

opened in 2009. owner: erin tavin
all major credit cards accepted

echo park >

What does it mean when you say somebody or something is a "true original"? Instead of putting it into words, just go to *Tavin* and meet the owner Erin. Shopping here is like being in the midst of an interactive art installation where the theme is Erin's vision of vintage. I think this place is perhaps the most expressive and intricately staged vintage shop I've come across; every piece is allowed to tell its own glorious story. Be sure though, when you visit, to give yourself enough time to browse, and then browse again. Soaking up the big picture is a wondrous journey.

covet:
tavin redesigned vintage
danceteria necklace
vintage:
  yohji yamomoto
  valentino
  boho batik
  christian dior
  comme des garçons

tenoversix

forward-thinking style

7427 beverly boulevard. corner of vista
323.330.9355 www.tenover6.com
mon - sat 11a - 6p sun noon - 5p

opened in 2008. owners: kristen lee, brady cunningham and joe cole
all major credit cards accepted
online shopping

mid-city >

"Ten over six" translates to ten shillings, sixpence—the price of the Mad Hatter's hat in *Alice in Wonderland*. Though you won't find anything for this lowly pittance in *Tenoversix*, you will absolutely find a collection of things as quirky and cool as that nutter, the Mad Hatter. And though there is no riddle here to solve, it's crystal clear that this store is full of amazing things to wear and carry. The only thing that dismayed me at *Tenoversix* was that there were so many things I wanted, my head was spinning like I'd just been on MH's teacup ride.

covet:
tenoversix tommy long
acne pop tote bag
anna sheffield earrings
slow and steady wins the race sweatshirt
loeffler randall yvette multi suede
filippa k laced boots
dieppa restrepo cali lace up
scout mushroom cap necklace

tortoise

artful japanese lifestyle store

1342 1/2 abbot kinney boulevard. between andalusia and navarre
310.396.7335 www.tortoiselife.com
wed - sun noon - 6p

opened in 2008. owners: taku and keiko shinomoto
all major credit cards accepted
online shopping

venice >

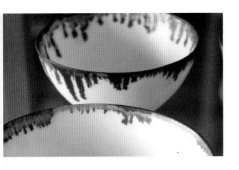

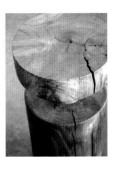

Though these days urban clothes horses think of the term "slow and steady wins the race" as a groovy clothing line, I think of the saying in conjunction with *Tortoise*. We modern folk often feel rushed to decorate and fill our homes, getting items cheaply and quickly instead of searching for things that will last longer but might take more time to source. For those steady sort of collectors, *Tortoise* is a mecca. Everything in this little store emphasizes quality over quantity and will remind you that patience, not speed, will serve you best in the end.

covet:
shiwa by naoto fukasawa
  string & button close envelope
marc newson cutlery
shigeki fujishiro stool
shoji morinaga wooden bowl
kiya knives
tea canister handmade in kyoto
kaname okajima pod chair

tortoise general store

general store for japanese goods
1208 abott kinney boulevard. between san juan and santa clara
310.314.8448 www.tortoiselife.com
tue - sat 11:30a - 6:30p sun noon - 6p

opened in 2003. owners: taku and keiko shinomoto
all major credit cards accepted
online shopping

venice >

Okay, everything I just said in *Tortoise's* blurb about being patient and about taking your time with your home and what you fill it with? Yeah, well, scratch that for a moment and come to *Tortoise General Store* and STOCK UP!! I kid you not. Hurry, because things here don't stick around for long. Taku and Keiko are constantly filling their mini-emporium with must-have-now pieces sourced from Japan and beyond. I think they should have named this sister spot to *Tortoise*, *The Hare*—but I will keep my nose out of naming and let my fingers do the buying.

covet:
colored paper tape
straw trivet
tenngui traditional fabrics
kono coffee dripper
stone handle bags
monkey hook
square head bottle opener
things for bread box

traveler's bookcase

a great little travel book shop

8375 west third street. between orlando and kings
323.655.1197 www.travelersbookcase.com
see website for hours

opened in 1991. owners: natalie compagno and greg freitas
all major credit cards accepted
online shopping

mid-city >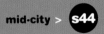

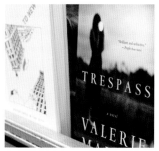

My husband Shawn is a voracious traveler. Every time he goes to a new place, he buys three guidebooks and two maps. I've even had to enact a rule that a plane ticket must be bought before a guidebook can be. But when I entered *Traveler's Bookcase*, the rules changed. In fact, if I would have had my suitcase with me, I could have had it filled in a minute flat—clothing and personal effects would have been jettisoned to make room for one of the best collections of guidebooks, maps and travel-related fiction I've ever seen. So Shawn, where are we going? Because I've got the guide for it.

covet:
guides:
  luxe
  city walks
  le cool
  eat.shop!
maps, maps, maps
this is rome by miroslav sasek
moleskin anything

zelen

antique, vintage and artful housewares
8055 beverly boulevard. between crescent heights and laurel
323.658.6756 www.zelenhome.com
mon - fri 11a - 6p sat 11a - 5p

opened in 2004. owner: mike andrews
all major credit cards accepted

mid-city >

Though I personally love a clean design aesthetic when it comes to home décor, I secretly admire homes where the owner has the flair to mix the slightly off-beat and obscure with more expected pieces. So when I walked through *Zelen*, my secret admiration grew and grew. Mike's got the knack for this look, and suddenly I wanted to throw out my whole clean and minimal thing and start over. But short of buying this entire store and installing it directly in my house, which sounds highly appealing, it might not be cost-effective at this moment. I'll just get a piece or two here, and start there.

covet:
zelen pearl martini picks
vintage bourbon, scotch & vodka bottles
wooden tree stump bowls
vintage corkscrews
jefferson mack hand-forged dice
framed agate & other findings by dan
cynthia sargent wool carpets
mussel bowls

189

zenbunni

curiosities, jewelry and chocolate
2307 main street. between strand and hollister
310.452.9605 www.zenbunni.com
tue - sun noon - 6p

opened in 2005. owners: bunni lezak and zen nishimura
all major credit cards accepted

santa monica > **s46**

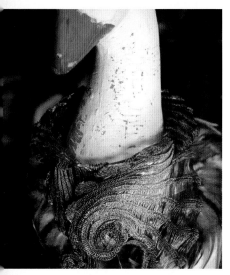

K: Zen and Bunni's businesses have been featured in all three editions of this book. I featured their short-lived, one-of-a-kind clothing store, *Elevator*, in the first edition. Agnes then featured the original Topanga Canyon incarnation of *Zenbunni* in the second edition. And now Anna is super excited about the new Santa Monica based *Zenbunni*. So though you may be wondering if we are getting massive kickbacks from this delightful couple, the truth is less sinister: these two are true originals and their businesses are also. You will see nothing else like this in town. Special is as special does.

covet:
jewelry:
  autumn macintosh
  lou zeldis
  shahlakareen
zenbunni raw organic chocolate:
  grey sea salt
  wild bee honey
zen's sculpture & bunni's photography

etc.

the eat.shop guides were created by kaie wellman and are published by cabazon books

eat.shop los angeles 3rd edition was written, researched and photographed by anna h. blessing

editing: kaie wellman   copy editing: lynn king   fact checking: michaela cotter santen
map and layout production: julia dickey and bryan wolf

anna thx: all of the business owners in this book. amy and david for a cozy place to stay and serious help with eating. annie for the much needed home-cooked meals and endlessly precise recommendations. shawn for always pushing for that third lunch or fourth dinner.

cabazon books: eat.shop los angeles 3rd edition
ISBN-13 9780982325476

copyright 2010 © cabazon books

every effort has been made to ensure the accuracy of the information in this book. however, certain details are subject to change. please remember when using the guides that hours alter seasonally and sometimes sadly, businesses close. the publisher cannot accept responsibility for any consequences arising from the use of this book.

the eat.shop guides are distributed by independent publishers group: www.ipgbook.com

to peer further into the world of eat.shop and to buy books, please visit: www.eatshopguides.com

PRINTED IN CHINA